CHESHIRE & DERBYSHIRE

Edited By Jenni Harrison

First published in Great Britain in 2017 by:

Young Writers
Remus House
Coltsfoot Drive
Peterborough
PE2 9BF
Telephone: 01733 890066
Website: www.youngwriters.co.uk

All Rights Reserved
Book Design by Spencer Hart
© Copyright Contributors 2017
SB ISBN 978-1-78820-234-3
Printed and bound in the UK by BookPrintingUK
Website: www.bookprintinguk.com
YB0321O

FOREWORD

Welcome to 'Crazy Creatures – Cheshire & Derbyshire'.

For our latest creative writing competition we invited pupils to write a saga inspired by a crazy creature. These creatures could be a mythical beast that just walked out a fantasy world, it could be an alien from outer space, it could be a creature from the darkest jungle or it could even be your household pet. Whichever creature had your imagination running wild we wanted to hear about it!

The challenge was tricky; pupils had to not only create a creature and a story around their creature they had to do it all in under 100 words! The pupils rose magnificently to the challenge and the stories we received were fantastic. As always the stories were of a very high standard, they were well written, engaging and humorous so I would like to congratulate everyone whose work has been included in this publication. I hope this competition has inspired you to keep writing and I look forward to reading more of your work in our future competitions!

Jenni Harrison

CONTENTS

Bradwell Junior School, Bradwell

Eva Amelie Nutting-Hughes (11)	1
Oliver Burton (9)	2
Emily Riley (10)	3
Megan Smith (10)	4
Harry Spencer (9)	5
Evie Ann Rose Sampson (9)	6
Lilly Greenan (10)	7
Eve Boyle (9)	8
Jake Astley (9)	9
Harry Eric George Lilley (10)	10
Max Bates (10)	11
Dylan Lawson (10)	12
Thomas Sambridge (10)	13

Bramley Vale Primary School, Doe Lea

Olivia Grace Thorne (9) & Hannah Louise Blake	14
Milli Angel McGurk (9)	15
Caiden-Lee Dawson (8)	16
Samuel James Kirk (8) & Riley	17
Luke Renshaw (9)	18
Lily May Roberts (7) & Holly	19
Maicey Stella Aspley (7) & Krista	20
Joshua Wright (8)	21
Dainton Jayce Cole Greig (8) & Kayce	22
Blake Michael Warwick (8)	23

Glebe Junior School, South Normanton

Jack Smedley (7)	24
Jessica Cook (8)	25
Sophie Smith (8)	26
Jessica Poyser (8)	27
Holly Mae Cooper (7)	28
Aimee Killen (8)	29
Nicola Parkin (8)	30
John William Agaba (8)	31
Grace Kimberly Allen (7)	32
Charlotte Rachel Sabin (8)	33
Felicity Khalsa (8)	34
Leo Cotterill (7)	35
Maisie Bridges (7)	36
Bailey Bowen (8)	37
Evie Smith (7)	38
Ellie Grayson (8)	39
Ruby West (7)	40
Harry Curtis (7)	41
Liam Anthony Morris (8)	42
Mia Hill (7)	43
Oscar David Renshaw (7)	44
Tilly Mae Wardley (7)	45
Kasey Elisha Fazakerley (8)	46
Caitlin Rose Cooke (8)	47
Nevaeh Hope Hickton (7)	48
Elisha-Rae Hurst (8)	49
Ava Wood (8)	50
Kate Robinson (8)	51
Lewis Jake Pritchard (8)	52
Kyle Johnson (8)	53
Jack Oscar Watson (7)	54
Warren-Lee Bowskill (8)	55
Connor Eric Phillips (8)	56

Macey-Lu Bettison (8)	57
Ayden Ludlam (8)	58
Emma Bramley (8)	59
Evie Ella-Rose King (7)	60
Alix Lee (7)	61
Kayden Gregory (7)	62
Joel Horsepool (7)	63
Mackenzie Clarke (8)	64
Lacey Lloyd (8)	65
Thomas James Potter (7)	66
Leah Bramley (8)	67
Jake Cooke (7)	68
Lauren Ruby Hyde (8)	69
Lexie Grace Gascoigne (8)	70
Taiya May Baker (7)	71
Josh Clarke (8)	72
Brett J S Taylor (8)	73
Laila Watkinson (7)	74
Joseph William Hoy (8)	75
Alex Oldfield (7)	76
Rocco Hardy (8)	77
Ruby Ball (8)	78
Euan Craig-Scrimshaw (8)	79
Amelia Jade Hall (8)	80
Louis Brammer (8)	81
Max Harrison (7)	82

Leighton Academy, Crewe

Eeshana Amit Naik (8)	83
Amy Marie Pointon (7)	84
Emily Palin (8)	85
Phoebe Rose Lloyd (9)	86
Erin Grace Lucas (9)	87
Chloe Louise Heath (9)	88
Christopher Southworth (8)	89
Teagan Angela Daniels (7)	90
Matilda Katelyn Scarlett (7)	91
Cameron Newman (8)	92
Tiffany Kelsey-Jade Lloyd (7)	93
Lydia Ella Frost (9)	94
Chloe Crystal Forster (8)	95
Lexi May Mellor (8)	96
Rubylee Rogerson (9)	97

Leon James Allcock (8)	98
Muhammad Hafeez (8)	99
Annabelle Marriott (8)	100

Longstone CE Primary School, Great Longstone

Joshua Joseph Leonard Orme (10)	101
Alice Elizabeth Chetwood (9)	102
Amber Pyke (9)	103
Ella Cox (9)	104
Imogen Lepski (10)	105
Hayley Jane Fairfax (10)	106
Cecily Hutchinson (8)	107
Ruby Pearce (10)	108
Noah Richards (9)	109
Tom Akeroyd (10)	110
Eva Thourgood-Marshall (9)	111
Spencer Thomas Simpson (9)	112
Connie Rowland (9)	113
Jens Frederick Heler (8)	114
Harrison Lawton (9)	115
Evie Bycroft (10)	116
Ben Priest (9)	117
Ned Heslop (10)	118

Manifold CE Academy, Warslow

Samuel David Bethell (8)	119
Evie Kate Bessant (9)	120
Molly Wardman (8)	121

Ripley Junior School, Ripley

Andrew Lincoln (8)	122
Georgia Cooper (8)	123
May Brown (9)	124
Isla Stevenson (9)	125
Phoebe Brooks (8)	126
Adam Taylor (9)	127
Madison White (9)	128
Cameron Borsley (8)	129
Rowan White (8)	130

Archie Swinscoe (9)	131
Kyle Haywood (8)	132
Amelia Elizabeth Gooding (9)	133
Alfie Jack Whysall (8)	134
Evie-May Spademan (8)	135
Ava Ford	136
Alfie Sissons (8)	137
Aaliyah Allen-Bell (8)	138

St Anselm's School, Bakewell

Elena Warrington Schwabe (11)	139
Ben Reeves (9)	140
Georgina Sheppard (11)	141
Tilly Gray (11)	142
Joshua Nuttall (11)	143
Olivia Jiménez (11)	144
Beatrix Larvin (11)	145
Colin Wilson (11)	146

St Luke's CE Primary School, Lowton

Sonny Phelan (9)	147
Alex Millard (9)	148
Ella Scott (9)	149
Caitlin Tegan Collins (8)	150
Louise Shepherd (9)	151
Benjamin Wu (9)	152
Tom Sofield (9)	153
Olivia Barrow (9)	154
Anna Winterbottom (9)	155
Catrin Norman (9)	156
Daniel White (9)	157
Christopher Friar (8)	158
Harry Owen (8)	159
Liam Bond (8)	160
Lucy Rava (9)	161
Noah Lewis (9)	162
Evie Cass (8)	163
Sophie Rava (9)	164
Sam Critchley (9)	165
Charlie Angus (9)	166
Albie Grimshaw (8)	167
Seb Scott (9)	168

Winster CE Primary School, Winster

Elise Gill (8)	169
Kitty Lee (8)	170
Bethany Bradley (9)	171
Jessica Webster (9)	172
Logan Brown (7)	173
Liam Crowther (9)	174
Kevin Webster (7)	175

THE STORIES

Potion Purple

Poka-Dot Paul is an ordinary three-eyed Spock-Dot. His squashy two-winged, purple body has orange spots on it. One day Poka-Dot Paul ventured into the depressed woods... In the woods Poka-Dot Paul saw a mysterious, deserted shop: Dingo Potions. *I must go in*, Paul thought. Wandering into the shop, Paul saw thousands of potions! He read the descriptions on some potions: 'Unicorn', 'Invisible'. Suddenly, something captured Paul's eye; a potion that read: 'Purple'. 'I must try this,' shouted Paul. Reluctantly, he opened the bottle and drank the potion. Suddenly, Paul's orange spots turned purple! 'Oh boy, I'm all purple!'

Eva Amelie Nutting-Hughes (11)
Bradwell Junior School, Bradwell

The Fight

One day, Eyeova saw Chuchu and they began to fight. *Bang!* Eyeova hit Chuchu in his many eyes! Next Chuchu hit Eyeover in his leg! Then Plonkidonk came. Then Plonkidonk and Chuchu were in an ambulance to go to hospital; Chuchu had broken his legs and his arms and Plokidonk had broken his spikes on his head. 'Ohhh!' wailed Plonkidonk and Chuchu.
Six days later Chuchu had died from a disease called the Black Death. 'I will miss Chuchu,' said Plonkidonk, 'I frequently saw him.'
'Me too!' said Eyeova. Then Eyova said, 'Do you want to be friends now?'

Oliver Burton (9)
Bradwell Junior School, Bradwell

Bluebobster's Nightmare!

As he wobbled about, Bluebobster sensed trouble, then he saw it... a water bomb flying, targeting his friend. Getting his extendable hair ready to cover him, he sprinted forward. *Splash!* It hit his hair. He gave Bluebobster a nod of approval and walked off. He saved his friends from accidents, but he could sense something more than trouble... danger! He saw it, an ice cream about to be dropped on a Perfectpink's hair, Bluebobster knew it would ruin her hair. Then he realised, 'I'm going to turn pink if I help!' But he grabbed her... *Bang!* 'Oh man, I'm pink!'

Emily Riley (10)
Bradwell Junior School, Bradwell

Enjai's Great Escape

Enjai, a young Jaspling, was on his daily excursion to find logs for his house. He was walking along when he stumbled into Agalgrii, the dreaded python. Enjai tried to fly, but some branches were in the way. It didn't help that he could hear more snakes coming eight miles away. 'I have you now!' Agalgrii hissed. Agalgrii was gaining on Enjai now. Enjai thought about his parents and how forlorn they would be if Agalgrii caught him.

Suddenly, Enjai, saw a tree. He climbed it recklessly then balanced on a very thin branch. Algalgrii hissed and slithered away angrily.

Megan Smith (10)
Bradwell Junior School, Bradwell

Grand Escape

The feared Demon Bicker is on the loose, with his five eyes, razor fangs, mohawk spike boots, leather jacket, demon wings, super sonic hearing and his tail. He bumps into Pizza Lord! Let the battle commence... *Ding! Ding! Ding!* Pizza Lord spits hot cheese, Demon Bicker uses motor cable, Pizza Lord does spice. *Slap!* Demon Bicker does a tail whip. Pizza Lord falls to the ground. His big mouth widens. He vanishes into burnt crust. Demon Bicker, with his spiky boots, stands on the crust. He's about to ride away when... Pizza Lord rises again. What will happen next?

Harry Spencer (9)
Bradwell Junior School, Bradwell

Untitled

It was a dark, stormy night just like this one and Zinglander was trudging through the mud. He was infuriated. It was mainly because he hadn't killed anybody or anything for the past few weeks and he was beginning to get a little agitated. 'Oogle Zing, a Blogging!' shouted Zinglanger. At that moment of time a blingdnding flew right past his purple, red-eyed face. Now Zinglander took this as a chance to finally kill something and started to chase it. All of a sudden, he fell slap bang into something. He realised it was his enemy Robah! 'Kill!' screamed Zinglander...

Evie Ann Rose Sampson (9)
Bradwell Junior School, Bradwell

Toast Disaster

There was a piece of toast, but not any piece of toast, a special one. He had pink hair (not normal) a moustache (definitely not normal) and he had four eyes. His name was Toastio. Toastio walked into the middle of New York and saw all the citizens as lively as ever. There was a huge clothes sale. He got as mad as the angry emoji and turned everyone into toast guards. Toastio saw monsters coming, they were his enemies. Flin-go and Blobby (Toastio's enemies) came and started fighting him. Unfortunately Blobby ate Toastio. They never saw evil Toastio again!

Lilly Greenan (10)
Bradwell Junior School, Bradwell

The Fight!

Fing-go walked along to the Prairie because he was meeting Blobby there. Blobby was Fing-go's BFF and every Friday morning they would meet up somewhere quiet. Then they would go to 'Poka-Dot Paul's Cafe' (which does the nicest pancakes. I would recommend it). Anyway, back to the story. So when they got there, instead of it being Poka-Dot Paul, it was Mr Tostio... Mr Tostio jumped out and fought with the two friends like nobody's business. He squeezed Blobby and Blobby fell to the ground. Now it was Fing-go vs Mr Tostio. The game was on...

Eve Boyle (9)
Bradwell Junior School, Bradwell

The War

One day there was a monster called Spikatron, who was from the space station. He was confident at everything apart from one thing: battling against his worst enemies, Demon Biker and Demon Rider, two close brothers who loved to fight together.
One day they all had a fight. Demon and Demon vs Spikatron. The fight went on forever, it took hours upon hours, upon hours. They all passed out apart from Spikatron, he stayed awake.
The next day Spikatron fell asleep for hours until his brother found him dead in his bed in the dead of night.

Jake Astley (9)
Bradwell Junior School, Bradwell

The Finding

One stormy, rainy night, a great, huge dustbin started to shake. Suddenly a boy, who had heard many stories of this haunted dustbin, walked past and decided to explore. He was wearing a really thick raincoat his nan had bought him. His name was Timmy. He had ginger hair and took a look inside. There was a big purple monster and he panicked so he took him home and hid him in his wardrobe, but then Timmy said, 'What will I feed him?' Anyway he fed him electricity and went to bed.
The next day the monster ran away forever.

Harry Eric George Lilley (10)
Bradwell Junior School, Bradwell

Untitled

One day an evil little monster came into town. He hated everyone. Whenever somebody tried to capture him he turned invisible and flew off somewhere. Nobody could hurt him because he was invisible. He had been stealing things from every shop in this town for months. Everybody wondered if he would ever be stopped. The next time he tried to steal something from the biggest shop in town, a superhero called Super Scary Spiky Spike came and tried to stop him. They battled everywhere, but... did Super Scary Spiky Spike ever defeat him?

Max Bates (10)
Bradwell Junior School, Bradwell

Untitled

One day Chuchu met Eyeova. Chuchu and Eyeova went motocross riding and Chuchu was good and Eyeova was bad. Eyeova fell off and broke his arms and legs. He had to go to hospital.

After six months Eyeova made best friends. The next day they went motocross riding and they were all good but ten minutes later Eyeova fell off and broke his arms and legs. Then he had to go to hospital again. After he came back from hospital he didn't go motocross riding again, only Chuchu went motocross riding...

Dylan Lawson (10)
Bradwell Junior School, Bradwell

Untitled

Crash! Boom! A tower falls. I fire my laser that I morphed my arm into. A human falls dead at my feet. I continue and fire again. I morph my other arm into a shield. I hop into my spaceship and I head straight for the mothership, destroying any enemy ships along the way. I head straight to the core and begin to fire. The core erupts in a huge ball of blue flame. The ship begins to crumble and fall. It heads down towards the main temple. The entire tentacle head race was nearly wiped out that day.

Thomas Sambridge (10)
Bradwell Junior School, Bradwell

The Forbidden Maze

Mysterious Midnight and Big Mouth were brother and sister, They loved playing chase in the beautiful sunshine. But once something went wrong. They saw grey smoke coming out of their neighbour's house. In a panic, they rushed next door but dropped down a deep hole... Argh! 'Ouch!' said Mysterious Midnight.
'Help!' said Big Mouth. They got split apart; and to their horror they were lost! In the distance, Mysterious Midnight could see a maze. On the other side Big Mouth thumped into a secret passage wall and the maze next to it. They both decided they'd go through the maze...

Olivia Grace Thorne (9) & Hannah Louise Blake
Bramley Vale Primary School, Doe Lea

Untitled

Bluebot was having an excellent day. He wanted to play football with his friends, Sandbot and Greenbot. Bluebot was doing kick-ups with the ball and scored the best goal ever! Bluebot, Greenbot and Sandbot decided to go on an adventure. They all went into the woods then they saw a massive creature lurking behind a tree in the woods! It looked like a colossal camel spider! It looked at the three boys and tried to eat them! They ran as fast as they could. Then they luckily found a green and hid in it. They thought it would go away.

Samuel James Kirk (8) & Riley
Bramley Vale Primary School, Doe Lea

Grrraham The Poisonous Dragon's Adventure

Grrraham was having a lovely day, flying around Creepy Cliff looking for food. Just then, he thought he saw something huge flying by. He looked again but could not see it. *What could it be?* he thought. He kept on flying until he saw a smaller dragon that he could eat. But just as he swooped down, he heard a swish! When he was brave enough to open his eyes, he was shocked to find he was in a larger dragon's mouth! He wriggled and shouted and eventually freed himself. 'Phew that was close,' he said as he landed.

Luke Renshaw (9)
Bramley Vale Primary School, Doe Lea

Clever Clogs and Rainbow Dragon

Clever Clogs and Rainbow Dragon were having a good day. They had just woken up and had three breakfasts and they were full up. They were both making sure their eyes were as straight as a giraffe's neck. They both saw a giant object! It was a funny looking colour like pink and purple. They thought it was a seashell. When they touched it, it made them disappear to the middle of nowhere. Luckily they did not drop the pink and purple seashell. They touched it again and it sent them back home where it was cosy.

Lily May Roberts (7) & Holly
Bramley Vale Primary School, Doe Lea

Untitled

One day, Tiny was walking to the beach, when suddenly he slipped on a banana and squished it. When he got up, he looked behind him and saw that the banana had changed into a giant monster! The ugly monster tried to stamp on Tiny, but Tiny was very brave and he threw a massive, shiny rock at him. To their amazement, the rock had magical powers and it turned the disgusting monster into a cute, fluffy cat! As quick as a flash, Tiny picked up the cat and took him home. Tiny now owns a lovely cat called Snuggles.

Maicey Stella Aspley (7) & Krista
Bramley Vale Primary School, Doe Lea

Untitled

Fargtoustic was waking up and saw a huge box of sweets in the middle of an old wooden house. He flew down the stairs and tried to grab it. Suddenly his four red and black wings gave way and he fell onto the hard, mucky floor. A few minutes later his wings were a lot better and he tried again. Smiling happily he jumped into the bright red and blue sweet box. When he was in the box, the box lid fell and he was trapped but happy because he could eat all the delicious sweets. Yum, yum!

Joshua Wright (8)
Bramley Vale Primary School, Doe Lea

Naughty

Naughty played with his football in the back garden. He looked up to the sky just as the titanic banana fell on him. He went to a strange place that was far away from his home. Looking over his shoulder, he looked behind him and thought someone was following him. He ran far, far away and got lost on a desert island. He saw a massive tiger, so he sprinted away and found a lion. He found a springy pad on the edge of the sea and he jumped so high that he bounced all the way back home.

Dainton Jayce Cole Greig (8) & Kayce
Bramley Vale Primary School, Doe Lea

Pancake Land

Dr Crazy was just having his pancakes in Crazy Land when he decided he wanted to go on an exciting adventure. He went to the Crazy Land forest. In the middle of the forest there was a pancake track that lead to a hole. He thought it was Pancake Land but when he entered... He was right! He started to eat houses, boats, the floor... he ate it all, so he got put in jail and got out. He was having so much fun until he fell into the hole that took him home.

Blake Michael Warwick (8)
Bramley Vale Primary School, Doe Lea

Blobby Boo

Sneaky, slimy Blobby Boo, who always says, 'Whodoo, you're very polite, you're very cute too! You are friendly. You are also tricky with your amazing tricks.' Everyone would be amazed and now, the best bit, Blobby follows you everywhere you go.
One day Blobby hiked into the woods that was made of sweets. How amazing was that? Just then, Blobby said, 'Oh, my eyes are nearly popping out.' Blobby explored and got lost. 'Oh no,' Blobby said, 'I'm lost!' Suddenly Blobby heard someone. 'Hello,' he said. They came closer... and closer... and closer... Yay! It was his mummy and daddy,

Jack Smedley (7)
Glebe Junior School, South Normanton

The Magical Shape-Shifter

The magical, marvellous shape-shifter monster was sneakily in the corner of a dark classroom, always changing shape! Changing and scaring, sneaking and creaking. The monster was always hiding. Suddenly, the green monster came out, scaring everybody in the classroom. The teacher looked into the shadow where the eye came from. The shape-shifter, who always changed shape, went to the corner and turned into hard rock. Suddenly he turned into a snail and he slowly crawled to the person's desk. Then he got his eye back and he showed everyone in the class all of his excellent tricks.

Jessica Cook (8)
Glebe Junior School, South Normanton

The Island Chase!

Furly was walking down the narrow streets of Fur Island. His furry, soft, feathery feet tickled the ground. Immediately, he looked at the huge notice board on a wall. One notice said: 'Be Warned, Enemies Coming!' Suddenly Furly's enemies, the evil monster gang, saw him and started chasing him. On his feet, he ran and ran and ran until he was lost in a part of Fur Island he didn't know. Then, another monster arrived with a shimmering coat. It was his friend, Puffy. Furly's power was to blend into coats. He blended into the coat and arrived home safely.

Sophie Smith (8)
Glebe Junior School, South Normanton

Cutey The Crazy Creature

One day a kid called Cutey was walking to his home. Cutey walked in and Cutey's mum said, 'I've bought your favourites.'
Then Cutey scanned the table. 'Noooo!' he screamed. It was his enemy, Pepperoni Pizza. 'No thanks I'll eat anything else.' Quickly, Cutey rummaged in his laundry. He sighed in relief, he'd found a T-shirt. He said, 'I'll eat this.' He ran to his room but instead ate his shoe. 'I hope no one will ever buy me a pepperoni pizza ever again!'
The next day he got pepperoni pizza again!

Jessica Poyser (8)
Glebe Junior School, South Normanton

Magnity

One sunny day, I was planting some flowers in the garden. But suddenly I heard a loud noise. It was a tall monster. He needed help because he'd walked so far that he didn't know his way back. 'Do you know where Monster Infinity Land is?'
'No,' I replied, 'but I'll find it!' I said. His name was Magnity.
'There's Monster Infinity Land,' Magnity shouted. There were hot chocolate stands, milkshake machines and a cinema. It was so good. I saw Mum coming, I rushed home and I got the watering can. Phew! Close!

Holly Mae Cooper (7)
Glebe Junior School, South Normanton

One Day In Zoopiton

One day a little fuzzball called Twizzles lived in a land called Zooplton. One day she was with her best friend called Chloe. One day they were swapping fuzfruit but Chloe would not swap, so she fell out with Twizzles. They missed each other lots. One day they saw each other and made friends again. They played together and made cakes together, they made a new friend called Squiggles, they all became best friends.
One day Squiggles and Twizzles went out together alone. Chloe got upset. Squiggles and Twizzles saw her and let her join in with the best fun ever!

Aimee Killen (8)
Glebe Junior School, South Normanton

The Adventures Of Cyclops

It was a hot, sunny day in animal land. Cyclops was steaming so he went into the shady forest. Then he turned into a bear and ran off. But then he heard a horrible squawking sound which filled the silent air. Cyclops didn't realise where the sound came from. But he heard a man cackle. Cyclops knew who that was instantly, it was the horrible Griffin. He ran like a bear, faster and faster and faster into the dark forest. Then he ran into Fluffy the Devil. He couldn't escape, he was cornered. *Oh no!* he thought, *will I survive?*

Nicola Parkin (8)
Glebe Junior School, South Normanton

Bonstoglermon's Battle

Bonstoglermon crawled out of his dark, shadowy cave. This was the first time in his entire life. Instantly his enemy, Augouion attacked him! Immediately Bonstoglermon fought back. He created an eye meteor by clapping his eye hands. *Boom!* Augoumon was blown up and Bonstoglermon thought Augoumon was destroyed... but he was alive, he had transformed into a... *rat*. Augoumon scurried into a hole in his rat form. Bonstoglermon crawled back into his cave, never to be seen again. He thought he would never see Augoumon ever again, but he was wrong...

John William Agaba (8)
Glebe Junior School, South Normanton

Untitled

One day Snicy Slither felt like there was something wrong. He wasn't at home in his lively bright Slitherland. He stretched his long forked tongue and licked the air for clues. *Where am I?* he thought. Suddenly his shimmering, patterned scales became as cold as ice. In the distance he could hear the deep and clonking sound. A bright red light came closer and closer. He used his distance eyes to see in the distance. He noticed there was a big, grey and angry robot. 'No!' said Snicy Slither. 'It's a robot.' Would he escape?

Grace Kimberly Allen (7)
Glebe Junior School, South Normanton

The Adventures With Gryffin!

It was a dark, shady day in Fang Land. Then Gryffin awoke. He was very unhappy. He decided to go to a party. He found a nice, sweet monster. He didn't like happy monsters! But when he got there he saw something, it was a notice board. It said: 'No Mean Monsters!' So he turned himself invisible so nobody saw him. Then he saw a nice, sweet monster, his enemy, he started running away. He turned himself invisible but Puffy could still see him! Gryffin said, 'Uh-oh!' Will he ever escape the nice, loving, happy Puffy? You never know!

Charlotte Rachel Sabin (8)
Glebe Junior School, South Normanton

My Naughty Monster Yamble

Once upon a time, there was a monster called Yamble. Yamble had an enemy called Ded Monster.
One day, Yamble went to the woods where Ded Monster lived to have a fight with Ded Monster. Yamble was the winner and Ded Monster lost, so then Ded Monster became Yamble's servant for ten years. Then Ded Monster became the king for four years but he had no servants. Then they both decided to have another fight. They both lost and both had to go to the hospital for their injuries that they had in the fight and they became best friends.

Felicity Khalsa (8)
Glebe Junior School, South Normanton

The Unexpected Battle

Flob crept and clawed his way through the school hall without any notice, leaving trails of slime all around the place. He was terrified if one of the children would see him! 'Wait!' Flob heard a creaking sound coming from the stairs. It was his enemy, Flurp... Flob got out his claws and scratched. *Smash! Clang! Smack! Scratch! Punch! Swipe! Crack! Smack!* Flob tripped up Flurp again. *Scratch! Clang! Punch!* Flurp was knocked out but now the children were looking at Flob! One of them said, 'Attack!' How will it end?

Leo Cotterill (7)
Glebe Junior School, South Normanton

Mr I Don't Like Pluto On Pluto

In the dark, dark spaceship, Mr I Don't Like Pluto was sleeping when his pet, Mr I Do Like Pluto wanted to go to Pluto. He crept to the rusty old engine then switched it on. He thought that it would be a nice trip. He zoomed off trying not to fall asleep because it was 2.00 in the morning. Suddenly they stopped. 'Yay!' Then Mr I Don't Like Pluto was on Pluto. 'Noooo!' He started stabbing Pluto. Then after an hour of stabbing he screamed. 'Argh! Help please!' Poor him. I'm sure he'll be OK eventually.

Maisie Bridges (7)
Glebe Junior School, South Normanton

Neil Armstrong

One hot day on Planet Mars there lived a person called Neil Armstrong. He transformed into a human. He was angry because he wanted to kill Deadpool and destroy Planet Bong. He said, 'I will defeat you Deadpool,' in a booming voice. He went to Planet Bong. When he got there he saw trouble. Deadpool was leading his army. This was the chance he wanted. He went through the army and killed Deadpool but it wasn't Deadpool, it was his commander. Deadpool came to him but Neil Armstrong killed him with his shiny and beautiful sword. Yippee.

Bailey Bowen (8)
Glebe Junior School, South Normanton

The Birthday Destroyer!

Puffy was going to a birthday party. When he got there it said: 'No Mean Monsters Allowed!' But Puffy was a kind monster so he went in. Happily he's at the birthday party and he's having a great time. Then he saw a face not familiar, so he got out his invisibility kit and put it on. It was a mean monster and he knew who it was. It was a mean monster called Griffin. So he said, 'A mean monster alert!' and all the people crowded round and bashed him down. Now he's leaving the party and meets Devil...

Evie Smith (7)
Glebe Junior School, South Normanton

Eyes The Alien

Far, far away lived a strange creature who floated safely on the moon. Eyes wanted to visit Earth because he didn't like the meteors or the black, dangerous, scary hole. So he floated to scary Earth. Just then he saw a weird object coming towards him. It was a rocket! A huge one. *Bang!* It hit him. He reached Earth. There were humans. He hated them. Eyes was in the corner of the classroom. The teacher shouted at somebody and moved them down the chart. Eyes went to the show and stole some pizza to celebrate. Yum! Yum! Yum!

Ellie Grayson (8)
Glebe Junior School, South Normanton

Rubarb

Once upon a time there was a bug that was called Rubarb the bug. He could do the splits and front flip. His enemies were Ruby's gems because they fought his friend. When they fought it was dark because it was midnight. Rubarb took a torch but sometimes his next door neighbour's light came on but the enemy couldn't see. If they held their ruby gem that meant the battle had started, when the ruby gem stopped glowing it was break but when it started glowing it started again. Rubarb won that battle, but sometimes Ruby wins.

Ruby West (7)
Glebe Junior School, South Normanton

Dumbydum's Toybox Adventure

Dumbydum lives in the toy box. He has lots of fun in the toybox. A few days later his worst enemy came and attacked. He and the creepy Hoover are worst enemies. 'Oh no!' shouted Dumbydum. 'I am going to have to jump out of the toy box.' So he did. 'Argh, Oos, ooh! That really hurts. I wish I could get back up into the toy box.'

Five minutes later: 'Oh finally I am back up into the toy box, time to attack. But first I have to wait. They were punching and kicking and Dumbydum fought to the death.

Harry Curtis (7)
Glebe Junior School, South Normanton

Adventure Of Deathray

Deathray was in a school. His black fur helped him blend in with the shadows. He knocked over a table and ran through the door. However there was something wrong. His arch-enemies were there. Some kids were in the long hallway. Deathray turned quickly into a locker. When he turned back to normal, he saw he was circled by teachers and kids. Deathray tried to get to his secret locker but the speedy teacher stopped him. He stretched his long legs and jumped over the small kids. Deathray hopped into his secret locker. So he could recharge.

Liam Anthony Morris (8)
Glebe Junior School, South Normanton

Wilson And The Dragon

One day, there was a monster called Wilson. He was walking to Sweet School with his friend. They ate candy at school and at the end of the day. Wilson slowly crept down the street, past the gingerbread house and down the gooey ice cream hill. Suddenly a dragon was at the bottom of the ice cream hill. It looked fierce and it breathed flames of fire. Wilson didn't see the dragon at the bottom of the hill and *gulp*, *burp*, Wilson was gone. 'That was nice said the fierce dragon.' Wilson was never seen again.

Mia Hill (7)
Glebe Junior School, South Normanton

Super Shape-Shifter gets Tricked

Super Shape-Shifter is looking really fierce with his arm gun out, his long whip-like antlers ready to strangle anybody near! Next he heard a human scream. That only meant one thing: Man Hunter! He sprinted towards the scream and he shape-shifted into a big brown box. Going forward he looked around... This was not his home. This was no classroom. He had been tricked. He was about to get sliced but he dodged and strangled one of Man Hunter's goons. He got out a sword and had a sword fight until his sword was broken. Oh no!

Oscar David Renshaw (7)
Glebe Junior School, South Normanton

Untitled

Once upon a time there was a kind witch and an ugly monster called Dead Monster. He was from Monster Town and he could breathe fire. His enemy was Yamble. The monster was an experiment gone wrong. It was supposed to be a kind monster and help people.
One day the horrible monster was back. Apparently one monster came every year. He destroyed the village, people screamed. The witch tried and tried but he was too strong so he created a potion really quickly and it worked and the monster was dead. She was so, so happy.

Tilly Mae Wardley (7)
Glebe Junior School, South Normanton

The Sadness Of Loony

In the deep, dark forest there was a monster called Loony. She saw a big forest so she went in and got lost. After that, she saw a group of dinosaurs, so she got eaten and her mum cried. Suddenly her mum heard a rumble and a tumble from the forest and she started rushing into the forest. The dinosaur was going to explode, so her mum stood back and... *boom!* The dinosaur exploded! Then Loony was back again! Yay! They went back home in the forest. When they got home, they celebrated Loony being back with lots of hugs.

Kasey Elisha Fazakerley (8)
Glebe Junior School, South Normanton

Calasoro And The T-rex

In the prehistoric forest, a malazor called Calasoro was going for a walk. There, stood in front of her, was a ginormous T-rex. The T-rex spotted Calasoro from the corner of his eye, so the chase began! The T-rex was right behind Calasoro when suddenly *snap!* Calasoro was trapped inside of the dinosaur's belly! Calasoro started to panic but then remembered what her friend, Eliot did. She began to tickle his belly! First the T-rex giggled, then he chuckled and he laughed out loud. Calasoro shot out of his mouth.

Caitlin Rose Cooke (8)
Glebe Junior School, South Normanton

Fierce Fluffy Devil Birthday Destroyer

Destroyer Devils are made up of clouds. Also, they are half human. He accidentally bumps into a mysterious magician. Suddenly, the Destroyer Devil turned into a red ball and secretly sneaked into the super food room. Just then Destroyer Devil ate all of the food. Can you imagine? Then, somebody was coming so then he turned into a red ball again. Secretly he hid behind a door all angry, lonely and red. What will happen next to Destroyer Devil? Happily Destroyer Devil saw a familiar face. It was Puffy, his worst enemy.

Nevaeh Hope Hickton (7)
Glebe Junior School, South Normanton

Meany The Mean Devil

One day a devil called Meany was walking in the bright, beautiful woods but then realised he was lost in the deep, dark woods, so he decided to walk on. But then he saw a big gigantic sandy town, so he went to the beautiful town. 'Please can you help me find my way back home?' he asked. 'So I could have some yummy pineapple pizza for dinner.' Some said yes, others said no, but one showed him the way back to his crazy, fun, naughty family. So they all had yummy pineapple pizza all together.

Elisha-Rae Hurst (8)
Glebe Junior School, South Normanton

Dynamite Dibby

One day a blaze came through the sky. It was in a forest where the sky lit up. A little alien popped out and said, 'Wawaw!' He was only little, well, a baby. He heard a noise behind him. It was a little boy. Dibby had never seen a boy before, 'Oh no!' said Dibby.
Dibby was scared but the boy said, 'Come in, I bet you are hungry. Have some chips.' Dibby just stared but then *zzzzz!* A noise in the forest. Dibby ran to his mother. 'Dibby!'
'Mjoither!' Dibby cried.

Ava Wood (8)
Glebe Junior School, South Normanton

The Spider Catastrophe

Googly Goo was green and round but only scared of spiders. He went out for a walk around his planet, Pluto. Googly Goo was shocked when he saw some spiders. He started to panic. The frightened monster was trying to think what to do. Then Googly Goo had an idea. It was a brilliant idea! He quickly jumped, pounced and then cartwheeled away. When Googly Goo went back he was very proud of himself. He wasn't sure how he did it but he was still very proud of himself. Googly Goo wasn't scared of spiders anymore.

Kate Robinson (8)
Glebe Junior School, South Normanton

Side Box

Once there was a monster. His name was Side Box. He was desperate to go to England, in fact it was his dream. Side Box found a fantastic map that showed where England was so he travelled forty miles. He met a gang who said, 'Go that way to England.' So he set off the way they'd said thoughtlessly. But he found out he was going the wrong way. He then went where the map told him to go. So now he's gone for miles. He thought, *I'm here*, but he found out that the map was fake. 'Nooo!'

Lewis Jake Pritchard (8)
Glebe Junior School, South Normanton

Jelly Wible Spike's Great Escape!

Far, far away, on the moon was a creature called Jelly Wible Spike. He had a super horn which had two brains inside, cat-like ears, mischievous, evil eyes. two poisonous tails and three spikes. One day Jelly Wible Spike was hunting for aliens. Suddenly, a rocket landed with three humans inside. They sneaked up on Jelly Wible Spike... and stole him... and took him to Earth! He escaped and he dashed away to a classroom. He hid in the corner. Just then, he got seen and he turned into a pencil and was never seen again!

Kyle Johnson (8)
Glebe Junior School, South Normanton

Mr Greeny - A Mini Saga

Mr Greeny is a good friend. He helps people if they are hurt. Mr Greeny is clever and strong. Quietly he lives in the dark, scary cave. Sadly he doesn't have any friends because he lives in a cave, but he does have two neighbours. They live next door to Mr Greeny and they go for a walk to play. When they get back to their dark, scary cave they have dinner in the cave. Then they hear a knock on the door. It is their enemy and he says, 'Hello.'
'Blobby get out!' says Mr Greeny. He is angry.

Jack Oscar Watson (7)
Glebe Junior School, South Normanton

Inky Stinky's Egyptian Adventure

Inky Stinky goes out and about. He goes to a different pyramid to see if it is empty to take some old things inside it. Then he sees some enemies so he attacks with his ink cartwheel and stink-out powers! Then he leaves to get his things. On the way he finds food. He finds three juicy apples to eat so he eats them. He's still hungry until another enemy comes but he says, 'You look hungry.' Inky Stinky nods his head and gobbles them up! Then he gets back home and sleeps and forgets about the pyramid.

Warren-Lee Bowskill (8)
Glebe Junior School, South Normanton

Untitled

Once upon a time there lived a spider underneath a bed. It had an enemy, a dish. It was really scary. Mum came in the room with some sweets on a dish. It was his favourite chocolate of M&Ms on top. So Tommy-Lee went to grab one of the M&Ms. Tommy-Lee stayed under the bed. Mum chucked the dish under the bed. Tommy-Lee was sick. Tommy-Lee was really sick and he was sick all over the room. The brother, Connor, went out of the room so Tommy-Lee came out from under the bed and got the sweets and ate them.

Connor Eric Phillips (8)
Glebe Junior School, South Normanton

Ricky And The Cave

Peeking up from the deep, dark sea, Ricky was very scary in the ocean. His eyes were green and shiny. Ricky could turn into a book and a pencil. He could do tricks with his hands. Ricky was in the cave, he was getting some sticks. It was dark. He became trapped in the cave. There was slime in the cave. Ricky said, 'Help!' Ricky's friend helped him but he was stuck. Ricky was scared of darkness. Suddenly, the cave door opened. He was happy, Ricky was free. He had a party with his friends.

Macey-Lu Bettison (8)
Glebe Junior School, South Normanton

Evil Killer's Football Adventure

Evil Killer was no ordinary creature. He was a killer but once he played football, he was brilliant. One night he ran away to Earth and he saw a poster. He thought he could find a football club. Then he searched and searched and found a football club on a massive playing field. He asked if he could join the football club, then he played a match against Good Pat. They were their rivals. They kicked off! The game started.
Fifteen minutes later they got a penalty which was saved. Killer scored!

Ayden Ludlam (8)
Glebe Junior School, South Normanton

Tickle Under The Table

Tickle was waiting for someone to walk by, but the mop came out and it got closer and closer. He ran out and tickled the mop until it fell over. Then he fell over and he noticed he was out of the table. The mop got up and sucked up Tickle. He got out of the mop and said, 'That's terrible.'
The mop said, 'Yes.'
Tickle got under the table and said, 'You cannot get me!' The mop tried to get under the table but he did not. Mop got put away forever and ever.

Emma Bramley (8)
Glebe Junior School, South Normanton

Blobby Sloppy Gets In Trouble

He has sloppy hair and horns like a bull. Blobby Sloppy has four arms. When he goes hunting he always gets into trouble, he always gets seen and mostly caught.

One day there was a massive storm and it blew Blobby Sloppy's ship away from the Monster World. When he reached the human world he saw something in the air. Then he realised it was a bunch of hawks surrounding him so immediately he ran to his ship and started mending it. When he finished mending it he quickly got in it.

Evie Ella-Rose King (7)
Glebe Junior School, South Normanton

Jenis The Alien

Once there was a boy who was having his breakfast. Then the pantry door opened and the boy's cereal went all on his head. He opened the door... it was an alien. The boy shouted. The alien said, 'Hello, shall we start with the kitchen?'
The boy said, 'Yes!' The alien ate all the food. Then the alien went to the boy's room.
'No!' shouted the boy. He got all of his pants out. Mum came back. Mum shouted loudly at the boy. 'Oh no!' said the boy.

Alix Lee (7)
Glebe Junior School, South Normanton

Bobbly Wobbly

Bobbly Wobbly is very, very strange because he has hair on his head and on his horns and he has a ghost's body.
Once Bobbly Wobbly travelled to the white moon but his rocket ship crashed instead of landing. He was fine. Just then a scared person visited, so he turned into a piece of the moon! But the person stayed too long and he turned back to his normal self and scared the person away meanly and that's why people don't go to moon. Would you want to be Bobbly Wobbly?

Kayden Gregory (7)
Glebe Junior School, South Normanton

The Mini Saga About Blobby

Blobby is very talented. He can turn into goo and can shoot goo out of his hands. One day he went on an adventure to Earth and landed in the forest. But it wasn't like his home planet, Uranus. He accidentally ran into someone called Ghosty. Suddenly Ghosty went to attack and Blobby got trapped in a cage. Blobby called Greeny to save him. Off Greeny went and Greeny found Blobby in a cage and sneakily saved him with a front flip and a back flip. Then they went back to Uranus.

Joel Horsepool (7)
Glebe Junior School, South Normanton

Untitled

Blob was just an ordinary alien. Blob travelled the multiverse looking for a sign to guide him back home to Planet Zigarde, but one day he was on the search for the sign when suddenly there was a shower of huge asteroids. All of a sudden one of them hit him and the ship got trapped. His worst fear. Evil Killer appeared before him. Quickly, he tried to capture Blob and he managed, but Blob managed to escape from his wrath and continued in his search for the sign.

Mackenzie Clarke (8)
Glebe Junior School, South Normanton

Untitled

As Bob wakes up with excitement, he jumps out of bed and runs as quick as the wind. He eats and chews as quick as ever. Then after one second he finishes all of his breakfast. Then he gets dressed. It is so hot and sunny. He decides that he wants to go for a walk. Suddenly he meets his enemy, Stewart the Spider. Bob screams and runs back home and says to himself, could my day get any worse? Anyway, Stewart the Spider didn't even catch up with Bob.

Lacey Lloyd (8)
Glebe Junior School, South Normanton

Untitled

Once upon a time there was a crazy creature called Euan. His enemy was a basketball because it bounced more than a football. Euan had skills like running fast and all around the world. Euan lived underneath my bed with my football and basketball but he stayed next to the football and not near the orange bouncy basketball. One day it followed him around the room and bounced on the bed and out the window. Euan won. 'Hooray!' he said.

Thomas James Potter (7)
Glebe Junior School, South Normanton

Living Under My Bed

Spotty lives under my bed. He eats lots of food under there. He is scared of dogs, cats and birds. He went to the park to play on the swings. He saw a dog and he ran back under my bed. He got home. He went to sleep and when he got up he went to the park again. He saw a dog again and said, 'It doesn't matter anymore, it is just a dog.' He went to play outside when Mum came in. He went crazy and someone found him under my bed.

Leah Bramley (8)
Glebe Junior School, South Normanton

Declan Under The Bed

Under the bed Declan was playing hide-and-seek. Then he got trapped in the toy box. Mum got him and chucked him in the bin. He couldn't get out! The lorry came and took him away. Suddenly he popped the bag and jumped out of the lorry. He was running back home and then a kid picked him up and took him away. His owner was fighting with the kid and his owner got him back home and they were playing a game on the PC.

Jake Cooke (7)
Glebe Junior School, South Normanton

Eaten

In the incredible park, Suctern was going for a drink. Suddenly he saw an angry dinosaur. Suctern started to slurp the dinosaur's drink. The dinosaur saw and chased poor Suctern. Suctern ran around the slippery slide. He dived in the yellow sand pit. He couldn't do it anymore. So he jumped up scared and ran speedily! He fell on the floor and got gobbled up by the wicked dinosaur. Now Suctern is dead.

Lauren Ruby Hyde (8)
Glebe Junior School, South Normanton

Super Strong Sam!

Tiptoeing down the wooden floor, Super Strong Sam came and ran away!
Oh no, a human came. He super quickly ran away. He ran outside into the forest and at last he was free! He ran back to Gobily Goo Goo Land with his friends. When he went back to the house, he realised that he could go into different shapes so when the human came, he turned into some coffee and a pencil. Finally, he got to run away.

Lexie Grace Gascoigne (8)
Glebe Junior School, South Normanton

The Monster That Lives Under My Bed

Crazy Apple lives under my bed. One day she breathed fire on my legs as I got up to go to school so I had to go to the hospital instead. When I got back, the week after, my mum had a cute baby who liked to go under my bed where the crazy monster lived. The crazy monster threatened her, but my crazy monster had to sadly move house to my next-door neighbour's house. She was not happy at all.

Taiya May Baker (7)
Glebe Junior School, South Normanton

Headbut's Adventures

Once upon a time there was a special meerkat called Headbut. He lived on Planet Mars. One day he decided to take a trip to Earth to meet all his meerkat friends. They had a fluffy party and he played a tune on his sax. Suddenly Tom the lazy cat sneaked up and tried to get the saxophone! But Headbut bumped him on the head with a bucket. Poor Tom had a huge bump on his head and he ran off like a baby.

Josh Clarke (8)
Glebe Junior School, South Normanton

Practice Makes Perfect

Did you know that there is a planet called Planet Guie and all the slimy people can go invisible except one slimy boy who cannot go invisible. His name is Blobble and he cannot go invisible. He tried and tried and he was worried that he would never be able to go invisible. Then one day his parents told him, 'Practise makes perfect.' So he tried and tried and tried. Now he can go invisible.

Brett J S Taylor (8)
Glebe Junior School, South Normanton

Jerry Under The Bed

Jerry lives under the bed. He bites people on the arm. Mum cleans under the bed. The Hoover gets closer and closer then suddenly he gets sucked up into the Hoover forever. He floats with the dust and bobbles and Lego. He is lonely. He gets a new friend called Freod. He is Lego. Then Mum gets him out. Then he goes under the bed again. With stinky Nikes and socks. His friend is lonely without him.

Laila Watkinson (7)
Glebe Junior School, South Normanton

Captain Underpants

Once upon a time there lived a really horrid captain called Captain Underpants. He was walking around on Planet Bong. Suddenly he saw his enemy Monkey Guy. Then they started to battle. Captain Underpants flew in the sky and shot lightning at Monkey Guy until he killed him. Suddenly, his pants flew off and landed on the moon. Captain Underpants lost all his magic powers and could no longer fight.

Joseph William Hoy (8)
Glebe Junior School, South Normanton

Joe Meme's Crazy Adventures On Planet Laserbeam

Joe Meme was on Planet Laser Beam when he was surrounded by his worst enemies, laser beam shooting chickens and the evil laser beam shooting chicken, Spanner Meme. He spawned laser beam chickens all around Joe Meme. He was trapped! What could he do? He used his laser beam against them. The chickens were defeated and Joe Meme happily walked back to Planet Laser Beam.

Alex Oldfield (7)
Glebe Junior School, South Normanton

Untitled

Once upon a time a creature named Gary was relaxing. Suddenly the Destroyer appeared and he nearly got Gary. But Gary air back-flipped into his face. In the end he got arrested by the police because he tried to kill Gary. Then Gary found his new enemy, Spider-Man. Gary was amazed. Spider-Man was slinging with his web-slinger.

Rocco Hardy (8)
Glebe Junior School, South Normanton

Untitled

Once upon a time there was an alien called Bubbles. His enemy was Ryhen. One day Ryhen came. Bubbles said, 'Hide!' but Ryhen found him. He got chucked in a prison. He got fed slop and drank slime. He had to work 15 hours a day. He was so, so tired. He only got two hours sleep a day and there were no games. He was so bored.

Ruby Ball (8)
Glebe Junior School, South Normanton

Gelling Trapped

Under the bed Thomas the creature got trapped in a box by Mum. She closed the lid while Thomas was in the box. Thomas was frustrated. Thomas was thinking of a plan to get out of the box. The box was plastic so he couldn't climb out. Thomas luckily escaped the terrifying mess and Thomas felt good.

Euan Craig-Scrimshaw (8)
Glebe Junior School, South Normanton

Pipa's Adventure

Once upon a time a monster was at home bored so she went to England. Her name was Pipa. She met the Queen and Big Ben but she hurt her eight arms. Suddenly she got snatched but someone helped her. She had been freed. She was very happy. Pipa and the little girl had the best time ever.

Amelia Jade Hall (8)
Glebe Junior School, South Normanton

Untitled

One day Meme was in his spaceship when he saw the Death Star full of chickens. He managed to get in. The weapon was nearly fully charged. He chopped the laser beam creator but he chopped his ship in half. How was he going to breathe? The laser shield saved him and he returned to home.

Louis Brammer (8)
Glebe Junior School, South Normanton

Franc's Worst Day

Once upon a time there was a monster called Franc. He was peeping over a rock. He lived in the sea. Franc saw in the distance, his worst enemy, Evil Frog. He was trapped in a cage. Suddenly his ear got chopped off. Suddenly he turned into a pencil then got home safely.

Max Harrison (7)
Glebe Junior School, South Normanton

The Lost Alien

Deep in the petrifying forest lived an incredible alien called Pong. After a week, hunters came to bravely hunt and carry the animals to the zoo. Accidentally Pong got into the bag which was supposed to put animals in. After an exhausted journey Pong was in the vast Marvellous
Zoo, surprisingly, he was with the misbehaving Gorillas. Confused and Miserable, Pong's brain had gone clumsy.
Pong sadly whispered, 'How can I get back to my precious Habbit?'
After a week, he sneakily popped into the airplane which was going to enter the rainforest. After he reached there he was ecstatic.

Eeshana Amit Naik (8)
Leighton Academy, Crewe

Doodle Plomp And The Gloop Monster!

Doodle Plomp ecstatically skipped across the rough, dirty path. Suddenly Doodle Plomp saw a vast spotty gloop monster. It was green with a variety of coloured spots. But the most frightening thing of all is how vast and green his mouth was. It was as big as a round mountain. Doodle Plomp spotted Horrid Holly on the slimy, sticky monster. As loud as thunder Doodle screeched, 'Help!' Doodle Plomp suddenly remembered what she had mastered at gym class. Surprisingly Doodle sneezed out of her fingertips which deactivated Holly of her powers and the gloop monster was never seen again.

Amy Marie Pointon (7)
Leighton Academy, Crewe

Laugh Time

Wiggle Love was a professional comedian, she loved making people laugh. Tomorrow was her big day to perform on stage. 'It's today, it's today!' she said. She was so excited as she entered the dressing room. The audience were shouting for Wiggle Love. She wobbled like jelly onto the stage then jumped up shouting, 'Boo!' Her wobbling body made everyone laugh. Suddenly her body started to change colour like a rainbow and her red heart-shaped eyes flickered. She swung a hula hoop round and round her arm. It was amazing until oops! It flew off her arms and crashed.

Emily Palin (8)
Leighton Academy, Crewe

Zilionbob The Hero!

Once there was a creature called Zillionbob who lived on Planet Google. Zillionbob was a very kind creature and helped everybody in his community. He had three incredibly googly eyes and colossal, terrifying horns. Suddenly, a horrific, dangerous earthquake struck on Planet Google. Zillionbob was knocked over but wasn't hurt.

Anxiously, the next morning he woke up and found that everyone had disappeared! Zillionbob found a solution, however, he had to use all of his legs by pulling everyone out of the centre of the planet. He took them to safety and everybody thanked him!

Phoebe Rose Lloyd (9)
Leighton Academy, Crewe

Oddtodd Gets Lost!

There was once a short, hairy and gentle creature, its name was Oddtodd. He had a warmhearted, ambivalent personality however, whenever he got angry he set on fire! Oddtodd's eyes suddenly got distracted by a swarm of bees coming by whilst Oddtodd screamed at the top of his small lungs. Suddenly, the bees started to pilot off on their way. As quick as a flash, Oddtodd remembered he had got lost because his ship had crashed! Straight after that he memorised what to do when he got lost. Use the compass. Not long after, he was able to navigate home!

Erin Grace Lucas (9)
Leighton Academy, Crewe

Batchesca The Bat

Dear Diary,

Today was a jolly good day because I majestically defeated Batman. I was spying on him all morning until I heroically jumped out of nowhere and attempted to bite him but I didn't quite get that far. Proud, I swiped my cape and glided through the murky sky. *Ping! Pong!* I had an out-of-this-world idea, I was going to gather a bat army! So that's what I did. I found Batman easy-peasy, Suddenly my bat army went to Batman without my command! I can't quite remember what happened next, but I was holding hands with Batman!

Chloe Louise Heath (9)
Leighton Academy, Crewe

Shadow Monster

One rainy night, in the Atlantic ocean people, were scuba-diving until a giant monster raised up with a deafening roar that shook the water. The scuba divers tried to swim away yelling as it stomped through the water. Then a 4,000m monster appeared to battle with the black shadow, they bit each other and the ocean turned red with blood. It was soon won when the black shadow ripped the boncrawler to shreds. The ocean was red with blood and calm after the battle. The black shadow then, in one breath of ice, froze the whole Atlantic Ocean. Battle over.

Christopher Southworth (8)
Leighton Academy, Crewe

The Sweet Competition!

'Roll up, roll up for the sweet competition: Bo-Bos against Do-Dos, now the team that can eat the most sweets wins... go!'
'I bet we'll win,' said the Do-Dos. The Bo-Bos didn't mind who won, they just wanted to eat the sweets.
'How are you doing Do-Do?' said the judge.
'Fine, sweets are nice.'
The competition ended, 'Now, the winner is... the Bo-Bos! Well done! And I have an individual winner well done Bo-Bo! Your prize is to become a Do-Do member! Well done Bo-Bo!'

Teagan Angela Daniels (7)
Leighton Academy, Crewe

Book Battle Bonk

Sparkeye loves reading so he goes to the library every weekend. One day when he came through the park Sparkeye heard a familiar voice from behind him. It was Cagecrang, he was a really nasty bully. He wanted the book because he didn't have a library card. Cagecrang bonked Sparkeye on the head with his own rock-hard head leaving Sparkeye with a huge bump. Sparkeye got sent to hospital. They tried everything on his bump, but the ice-pack melted because it was so warm, so off to Pluto where it was colder for poor Sparkeye.

Matilda Katelyn Scarlett (7)
Leighton Academy, Crewe

The Burp

One day Greebie was wandering down a deserted road. Just then he swerved around and saw a load of spiders trying to capture him. He tried to run but he got caught in a web. The spiders caught up with Greebie and took him back to their secret lair. When they got there the spiders hung Greebie on a wall and went off. Without thinking, Greebie used the chainsaw on his back to cut the chains. When he ran off he bumped into two spiders, they caught him and he did a tremendous burp and twenty-five thousand hot dogs came out!

Cameron Newman (8)
Leighton Academy, Crewe

Daisy The Naughty Mermaid

One sunny day Daisy was swimming around the ocean when she met a nasty fish dragon called Thunder.
Thunder took Daisy away from her family and Daisy didn't know where she was going. Daisy's family wondered where she was because she hadn't been in so they went out to look for her, but it started to get dark. It was very scary in the ocean at night so they returned home. Daisy got away from Thunder and she got caught up in fishing wire. It was a fisherman who caught her and took her back home to her family.

Tiffany Kelsey-Jade Lloyd (7)
Leighton Academy, Crewe

Kilo's Terrible Nightmare

One day a monster called Kilo was wandering around on an adventurous planet called Planet Dong. He was off to see his best friend called Amen. It was a very sunny day so he decided to ask Amen if they could get a swimming pool out. When he got to Amen's house he saw that there was a tornado coming their way. Kilo rushed inside and warned Amen but it was too late, they were blown away by the tornado. When the tornado stopped they were in a very different world to theirs. It was an amazing, fantastic, wonderful place.

Lydia Ella Frost (9)
Leighton Academy, Crewe

Scary Gets Lost

Once upon a time there was a creature called Scary. He really didn't like humans at all. One day, Scary went walking in the forest and got lost. 'How can I get home again?' So he had to sleep there. In the morning Scary had no breakfast so he just ate leaves. Scary wasn't scared of anything, but today he was scared. It was nearly dark and Scary needed to go home, so he set off. First he turned left, then right. Then he finally got home safely but was very hungry when he got home. Very, very hungry.

Chloe Crystal Forster (8)
Leighton Academy, Crewe

Minnie's Travels

Minnie excitedly ran to school in the morning. But her teacher was not in because she'd hurt herself. Minnie was so, so upset. Minnie went outside to play. But it was so slippy that she fell over and broke her arm and she screamed because it hurt that much. Then Mrs Sayer, another teacher, helped Minnie to the hospital. They bandaged her arm up and then they went back to school, but Minnie really wanted to go back home. So Mrs Sayer let Minnie fly back to space in a big rocket. She loved it so, so much.

Lexi May Mellor (8)
Leighton Academy, Crewe

Cranky's Miserable Birthday!

Once upon a time there was a planet called Plantalot. On that planet it was a very good day for Cranky the alien because it was his birthday. All of his family were celebrating it. They all gave him presents which he really liked. But what he really wanted was to go and see the humans' style. So that night he sneaked out to go and see the humans. When he got there he was so angry that he ended up killing them. But then his mother came and took him home. He was grounded for a week. What!

Rubylee Rogerson (9)
Leighton Academy, Crewe

Pluto

Blobster was playing with his friends. He was showing off. He showed them that he could transport place to place and he said he was about to go to space. He found himself stuck on Pluto, home of his worst enemies. One walked up to him and said, 'Hey do you want a fight?'
'Go on then,' said Blobster. So he got his long tongue and wrapped it around him and threw him off the planet. 'Finally I've got myself free, ha, ha home at last!'

Leon James Allcock (8)
Leighton Academy, Crewe

Ant Man And The Five Star Hotel!

Ant Man was strolling along the big broken road, he was looking for a job he had tried everything but nothing had worked for him. He looked there, he looked here, but he didn't find anything. Suddenly in the distance he saw something. He went closer to it and saw a five star hotel. He went there! Darfader stopped him but because Ant Man was small he walked straight past him.

An hour later Ant Man was happy because it was the perfect job for him.

Muhammad Hafeez (8)
Leighton Academy, Crewe

Batman Forever

Once upon a time there was a bat called Batman. He flew across rivers and trees. He ate fruit and burgers for breakfast everyday. He pecked on trees. He ate slime for tea. There was a dragon who was watching him and the dragon decided to chase the bat with fear out of the country to China. He met new friends in the pub and drank beer with his new friends. He also helped people.

Annabelle Marriott (8)
Leighton Academy, Crewe

Untitled

It was twelve lunchtime on a Friday. The clock in class four banged and bonged at twelve noon. Clocktoe burst out of the clock. 'Argh!' screamed the children.
'Argh!' screamed the teachers.
Clocktoe shrank down and jumped into Josh's digital watch. Josh's watch bleeped and the numbers started rolling. Josh looked at his watch and Clocktoe puts his head onto the screen. 'What's wrong?' asked Josh.
'I don't like twelve o'clock bangs,' said Clocktoe. Everyone looked at Josh's watch. 'No problem,' said Josh and turned off the bangs on the clock. Clocktoe thanked Josh and stayed to teach about time.

Joshua Joseph Leonard Orme (10)
Longstone CE Primary School, Great Longstone

Monster Music!

As Twinkle Toes reached the venue, he stood in shock, like a long slithering snake, the queue stretched for what seemed miles! Finally Twinkle Toes reached the desk. 'Name?' The grumpy lady asked.
'Twinkle Toes,' he replied proudly, 'and I've got the monster music in me!'
The clock ticked by slowly. Sweat dripped off Twinkle Toes like a tap with a leak. 'You're up,' a voice shrieked. The music started, Twinkle Toes began to sing.
'Wow'! Music Mentor Slivery Simon replied. Twinkle Toes' career went from strength to strength. He smashed the Monster Music charts. Twinkle Toes was a star!

Alice Elizabeth Chetwood (9)
Longstone CE Primary School, Great Longstone

Zaxin's Adventure

One day in a land far, far away, Zaxin the chameleon was out for his daily stroll. Suddenly it started to hail. *Oh no!* thought Zaxin, because he knew what hail did. It meant that he couldn't camouflage himself since hail was frequently moving. So he just turned blue and sat there listening to the crashing hail. But then a dark bird-like figure started to rush towards him. Zaxin didn't know that, actually, the black figure was his friend. Matt scared. Zaxin screamed, not knowing what to do then!
The figure took off his outfit and said, 'Hey, wanna umbrella?'

Amber Pyke (9)
Longstone CE Primary School, Great Longstone

Fang's Frightening Find

Fang is my favourite pet Alien. He is seriously scared of Scorpions! He has five sparkling silver eyes, arms all wriggly like spaghetti and he has hair like a beautiful peacocks tail. Once, when playing football, Fang felt a strange pebble-like object moving in his best trainers. He jumped up and down repeatedly, screaming, trying to violently kick off his annoying shoe. With that, Fang's uncomfortable trainer flew through the air, landing in a massive, light brown, smelly camel pat. From that day on, Fang always checks his shoes carefully by tipping them upside down and shaking them gently.

Ella Cox (9)
Longstone CE Primary School, Great Longstone

Crackly Sloop's Cereal Box Adventure

Crackly Sloop is a cereal box prize.

One day he was poured onto his enemy Cheerio Strong. Suddenly, they had a fight about who was stronger. Crackly decided to be kind and let Cheerio Strong be the strongest. They are still enemies. Both of them had wives. They lived in separate boxes luckily. Otherwise, um well... let's say they wouldn't get on.

One day, Crackly went on a walk to the riverside. He bumped into Cheerio. They were both devastated, they ignored each other. Crackly got home and thought what good friends they could have been. Cheerio thought that too.

Imogen Lepski (10)
Longstone CE Primary School, Great Longstone

The Story Of Angry-Rosalina

One day there was a crazy creature named Angry-Rosalina. Every time someone entered the room, she went up to them and attacked them. A mean, horrible girl came in, but Angry-Rosalina stayed where she was because she was too scared to go out. The girl thought it was boring, so she decided to walk out. Next, two more kids came in. The crazy creature came out. She thought they were kind, Angry-Rosalina asked their names. Their names were Annabelle and Sophie. They were besties. Angry-Rosalina wanted to be their friend, so she asked. She was allowed to become Happy-Rosalina.

Hayley Jane Fairfax (10)
Longstone CE Primary School, Great Longstone

The Unfortunate Carlic

Carlik was a sour little garlic. He was having friendship troubles. He was with a beetroot but they broke up with each other. She went off with another beetroot. So since then beetroots were his worst enemy. He wanted to be with the glamorous carrot called Ada. The trouble was Ada found Carlik dumb. He decided that the best way through this was to become evil. He was going to plan something so sour that she would have to be his friend. But... it doesn't work. He was put on a rotten vegetable pile, where unfortunately he was never seen again!

Cecily Hutchinson (8)
Longstone CE Primary School, Great Longstone

Mr Cheerio Strong's Cereal Box Adventures

This story starts in a cereal box where Mr Cheerio Strong was with all of his Cheerio friends when up marched Crackly Sloop. Suddenly they got poured into a big bowl and an unexpected splash of milk fell down. For the second time he marched up to his enemy Mr Cheerio Strong. They had a big fight. Mr Cheerio Strong used his lasso to swing rice crispy sloop around in the air. He said, 'Please stop!' They said sorry and shook hands!
One day they bumped into each other in the family dishwasher and they decided to become best friends.

Ruby Pearce (10)
Longstone CE Primary School, Great Longstone

The Hairy Beast Of Glenrothes

This is the story of the Hairy Beast of Glenrothes', whose real name was McFluffy.
One night, he came into town to steal the dinosaurs from all the roundabouts. A police inspector saw McFluffy and tried to run away as fast as he could. McFluffy managed to get into the sewers without being stopped. Each night you could hear him roaring through the drains. The people of the town could not sleep because of the noise he made and soon they were able to capture him. A lorry came and took him to Edinburgh Zoo to be happy.

Noah Richards (9)
Longstone CE Primary School, Great Longstone

The Nuclear Error

In Hiroshima, in the most radioactive spot, was a huge error. It created an amazing and strange thing, a creature... The creature had one eye, a huge belly and two super skinny legs. When he got out of Hiroshima he wanted to see the world. So he went to Tokyo airport and scared everyone out. He went to Africa, Russia, Australia, and last but not least England, and decided to go to one of the school's because he was extremely hungry...
And when he got to my school he couldn't get enough of it, so he went to yours too.

Tom Akeroyd (10)
Longstone CE Primary School, Great Longstone

Bubbles Flies

When Bubbles was born in Turtur Land she was not a normal or ordinary turtle.
She was a turtle with a difference. The difference was that she had wings.
One sunny day, Bubbles decided to try and fly. So she found a cliff to jump from. The drop wasn't too deep down or too shallow. She jumped and flapped her wings. She flew over valleys and over rivers until she was distracted by a bird and she crashed into a tree. The bird flew down to help Bubbles up. After that they made friends with each other and flew away.

Eva Thourgood-Marshall (9)
Longstone CE Primary School, Great Longstone

Tattletail, Tattletail

One day Bing and Bong wanted to travel to Earth so they set off. When they got there, they needed to get a car so they hired one. They broke the speed limit and caused a lot of damage. All of the police pulled them over and told them off. They said they were sorry and promised not to do it again.

Later that day they did it again but this time they did something else. 'It was all his fault,' Bong said. 'No! It was all your fault,' Bong said.

Today they still fight about it everywhere they go.

Spencer Thomas Simpson (9)
Longstone CE Primary School, Great Longstone

Untitled

One bright day, there was a one-eyed monster in my kitchen window. I went in and said, 'What is your name.'
He said, 'Splodge.' He trudged along on his ski-like feet and started talking. But as time went my parents were home and I had to hide Splodge in my room otherwise Mum would send him away. A few day's later my friend, Ella, came round. I told her about Splodge and we all went and played outside. Splodge was amazing. He had magical powers. Sadly he had to go back to Zoo Land.

Connie Rowland (9)
Longstone CE Primary School, Great Longstone

Billy Ballo's First Pull

Billy Ballo had finally gotten a hobby and it was pulling people down the loo!
One day he tried to get his first pull but he failed, lost his stool hat and got flushed back down. So Billy Ballo planned revenge.
One day, Mrs White went to the loo. She reached for the handle to flush but just before Mrs White pulled the handle Billy Ballo grabbed Mrs White's hand and pulled her down the loo. Just then Mr White walked in, jumped in the loo and tried to save his wife but got stuck, forever and ever again!

Jens Frederick Heler (8)
Longstone CE Primary School, Great Longstone

Untitled

One day there was a little monster called Cyclops. It was his first day living at school. Cyclops lived in a little corner. He lived in the corner because the teacher could not see him, but the children could. The children got scared of him, so he needed to stay hidden.

One day, when he wasn't living at school, there was a bunch of children and two adults. The children saw him and got scared but the adults didn't know what the children were getting scared for. Cyclops got away so he could get home to Mum.

Harrison Lawton (9)
Longstone CE Primary School, Great Longstone

Sweet Dreams

It was going dark and Derp was hungry. He had been flying for a long time until he found a small village. He needed to find people that were asleep so he could eat their dreams. He heard snoring coming from a house, so he flew in to have a look. He found a huge sleepover party and thankfully everyone was asleep.

Some dreams were disgusting and some were lovely and sweet. Some were so big he couldn't finish them. He was so full, he fell asleep until morning. He is still living at the same house today!

Evie Bycroft (10)
Longstone CE Primary School, Great Longstone

Fuffy And The Meenie

Fuffy was a pink ball of fluff with one eye. He lived on the planet Nethare, the 150th planet from the solar system's sun.

One day he was at the park, when he saw a meenie (a bully in English) and said, 'Stop being mean!' He challenged him to a race. Fuffy won and the meenie was not mean anymore.

Then his dad said, 'No dessert!' Now Fuffy liked dessert, so he grew really big and ate his dad. Now he could have nice desserts whenever he liked... and he did until he got fat!

Ben Priest (9)
Longstone CE Primary School, Great Longstone

Terror Of The Sea

One cold misty morning a fisherman was out at sea. He was rigging up his gear, getting ready for a big catch. He threw out his net and when he pulled it in, he found some mysterious fish in the net. He got his hook to the line, then got the fish as bait. He threw a massive cast. Immediately, a huge, strong, fierce monster fish jumped out of the water and turned and smashed the boat with a long tusk. Frightened, the fisherman cut the line, racing to the wheel to speed for home.

Ned Heslop (10)
Longstone CE Primary School, Great Longstone

Sticky Tongue

There was once a spider whose tongue could stick to anything. He only found out when he tried to eat raisins. One day he went on a race and he didn't really race, instead his tongue dragged him. His tongue dragged him through hills, woods and swamps. Suddenly his tongue went dry and didn't stick anymore. The spider ran and ran until he couldn't run anymore. Sticky Spider felt his tongue. It was sticky again. He put his tongue on a car and got a lift to the end of the huge race. He won a hundred pounds.

Samuel David Bethell (8)
Manifold CE Academy, Warslow

Zogbarge Delivers Victory

Zogbarge was a terrifying monster who went to Monster High in Leek...
He was a nice little monster but no one liked him and he was always bullied.
One day he saw on the news that his planet was in danger. His family was rich, so he bought a spaceship. Next, he built up a crew to go with him. The news said that someone was going to smash his planet. Zogbarge and his monster crew fought them off. It was a gruesome battle but Zogbarge won. They were never to be seen ever again and Zogbarge became a hero.

Evie Kate Bessant (9)
Manifold CE Academy, Warslow

Book Man Tries To Take Over The Library

In the library, there was a book, a very mean book. When children read it, it magically wrote things that it wanted the children to do. It had gotten loads of children expelled.

The next day he held a meeting at the back of the bookshelf. Bookman said, 'I am planning to take over the library, I have already taken over one quarter of it.' But suddenly, there was a flash of light... 'Oh no!' He forgot the bookshelf being moved, then a person saw him talking and put him in the bin.

Molly Wardman (8)
Manifold CE Academy, Warslow

The Magic Star!

Spike shot through space on his spike rocket trying to find the magic star. Suddenly, Spike heard a strange noise coming from the engine. In the blink of an eye the rocket shattered into pieces.
Suddenly, Spike found himself on Earth; he saw the star next to him, grabbed it and went for a walk.
'Boo!'
'What was that?'
'Ha! It's me from Spikekind!'
'Hello Fluffy!'
Spike told Fluffy about his rocket. Spike and Fluffy fixed it and they went home with the star to make the shield around the land. Spike and Fluffy were happy with their grand achievements.

Andrew Lincoln (8)
Ripley Junior School, Ripley

A Clean Adventure

One hot morning, Sneezle was being nosy as usual. He was just peeping through Mrs Snake's window when something most peculiar happened. He was teleported to a world that was all clean! He wandered around only to find some people. He went to say hello when one of them said, 'I hope our soldiers defeat the Snatigons.'
Oh no! thought Sneezle, *I want to go home.*
As he was daydreaming the Cleanies had captured him and took him to their leader. He said, 'We will wipe your kind off the face of the Earth, prepare to be demolished.'
'Oh snotballs!'

Georgia Cooper (8)
Ripley Junior School, Ripley

Rainbow Sprinkle And Her Cupcake Friend

One morning, Rainbow Sprinkle was covering up her cupcake friend with sprinkles, when suddenly the dark night appeared! Rainbow Sprinkle teleported herself and her cupcake friend to somewhere neither of them had ever been before... The Land of Darkness! Rainbow Sprinkle had a plan but her cupcake friend did not know what to do! With no time to waste, Rainbow Sprinkle dashed off to the king's castle. She had only just managed to squeeze through the keyhole and rush to the Globe of Darkness. Then she rained sprinkles onto the globe and turned all darkness into cupcakes and dreams.

May Brown (9)
Ripley Junior School, Ripley

The Adventure Of Phoebz

Thud! Phoebz landed on the ground bruised and confused, she instantly knew this was not her home, Candyland. Being half-dog, half-marshmallow, she struggled to get her back up on her feet. However, once up, she felt the sugar rush around her body. Her energising powers began to kick in, she knew she somehow had to get home. But how? Suddenly she heard snarling and felt something nibbling on her leg. Looking up, she realised, it was a pack of hungry dogs. With lightning speed she ran for her life. 'Argh!' Could this be the end of Phoebz? Who knew!

Isla Stevenson (9)
Ripley Junior School, Ripley

The Revenge On Molly The Honeydew Melon

Finally, the fridge door had closed for the night. She could now get Molly back for throwing seeds at her last night!

Milly made her way around the fridge, knocking things over and making a mess as she went. She was in a hurry to get her Molly back.

Then Milly said, 'Ah, ah, ah! She's asleep so I can take revenge back on her for what she did last night.' Milly pulled out her chilly-o-matic shooters and kept hitting Molly with them. Then with the biggest of grins, Milly chuckled her way back to her cosy and comfy settlement.

Phoebe Brooks (8)
Ripley Junior School, Ripley

Untitled

Charlie trotted along the hard surface of the moon. Reaching his telescope, he gazed at the Earth. He saw sad children and wondered why. He wanted to cheer them up, so he flew to Earth. The children were surprised to see Charlie, the fluffy blue creature with four arms and three legs. The circus was close by, but it looked boring. Charlie knew he could be the world's best juggler because he had so many arms. He joined the circus to entertain the children with all his brightly coloured balls. The children cheered loudly and begged him to stay forever.

Adam Taylor (9)
Ripley Junior School, Ripley

Crazy Saga

Marzie is a monster, she is blue with yellow spots, she has five eyes and his very hairy and fluffy. Marzie is a good monster. She does gymnastics, helps people and is very kind and gentle. She has a pet cat. Marzie loves animals. The animals are sometimes scared of her because animals don't know what monsters are. Marzie's favourite food is fruit. The cat doesn't like fruit. Although it likes meat and fish. Although cats are scared of Marzie, they still enjoy playing ball together. When the day is done, the cat likes snuggling up to Marzie.

Madison White (9)
Ripley Junior School, Ripley

One-Eyed Stinky Winky And The Smelly Pond

It was a hot day and One-Eyed Stinky Winky went to his favourite place, a pond which no one knew about. Or so he thought. Stinky Winky was minding his own business bathing. He heard some rustling in the bushes, 'Who is there?' he shouted.
'It's me Mr Clean. Why are you bathing in that pond?' he said. 'You will stink, the pond is full of muck! Use this fresh water out the house pipe, that way you will have more friends.'
Stinky Winky smiled and said, 'Thank you for your kind help.'

Cameron Borsley (8)
Ripley Junior School, Ripley

Bing's President Adventure

Bing left Planet Bong looking for food. He wasn't concentrating and got lost, so lost, that he was at the other side of the solar system. He saw a blue and green planet and landed there. He was rubbish at landing his spaceship and crashed straight through the roof of the White House where Donald Trump lived. Trump locked Bing in prison. Bing knew he had to escape. When the guard came, Bing squirted him with ink and used his long horn to crush the bars and escape. He teleported to his spaceship and went home, still feeling very hungry.

Rowan White (8)
Ripley Junior School, Ripley

Lost In Space

One sunny day, Jeffery flew into space from Minneapolis America in a spaceship. He was desperate to see what was in space. He saw an alien. He ran and ran, but the alien caught up with Jeffery every time he started to try and run away from the bleeping space alien. At midnight the spell on the rocket would break if Jeffery didn't get back to his rocket and he'd have to stay there forever. It was midnight and he went to his rocket on Planet Jamie. He realised something was missing... it was his rocket! What would he do...?

Archie Swinscoe (9)
Ripley Junior School, Ripley

Fuzz's Invisible Adventure

Fuzz walked on a tiny path. It was dark. He loved the dark, it was his favourite. He flew in the air and when he looked down, he was frightened. When he looked down he hurt himself. He was OK.
He pressed the invisibility button and turned invisible. No one could see him and then he went somewhere where he wasn't allowed to go. Then he pressed the button again and then he turned visible and everybody could see him. They said 'hi' as they walked past and he said 'hi,' back as he walked past.

Kyle Haywood (8)
Ripley Junior School, Ripley

The Creepy Wood

One day there was a monster called Rokow. He went to the forest and the monster found a path and followed it and he found some fruit. He called it Olag, but it was actually called an orange. He ate it and then he had grown. He wondered what made him grow. He said, 'Oh the orange had a spell on it.' Then his enemy too came over with some lasers and some light gases too. Rokow was scared what was going to happen? Then he shouted, 'Oh no, he's coming to hurt me.' He then got saved eventually.

Amelia Elizabeth Gooding (9)
Ripley Junior School, Ripley

The Myth Of The Lake

One day, Dino Bird was playing tig but suddenly he sensed his worst enemy, Fire! The reason he hated Fire was because his head was made of TNT, so if it was set fire to, he would blow up. He took a quick look at the fire but before he had looked, he was on fire. He rushed to the lake. He went faster than he had ever gone before, but did he reach the lake in time? Nobody knows... All I can say is that, every night the lake explodes with impressive fireworks which crash and bang all night long.

Alfie Jack Whysall (8)
Ripley Junior School, Ripley

The Monsters Of Three Stump Island

There were three friends sailing on a boat when it sank. They swam to an island. On the island there was a stump, it had a carving of a hippo, a crocodile and a pig. The island was called Hippacrocopig. At first the friends were scared of the monster, but in the end they found out he was friendly and he helped them build a new boat to get off the island and back home where they told everyone about the magical monster and three stump island. The people of England didn't believe them though.

Evie-May Spademan (8)
Ripley Junior School, Ripley

The Life Of Luna Moon-Kitten

Luna had a life of peace and quiet. She loved how her house was soundproof.
One day, she had a problem, she was a human! She was in the human world as well! She saw a school and went in... Everyone was like her. It was incredible. She met some lovely people. They let her join their club. At the end of the day she just got out of school and her sister was there. Her name was Luna Moon Puppy because her mum was dog and her dad was a dog.
Her sister bullies her so she fought back.

Ava Ford
Ripley Junior School, Ripley

Alftron Escape

Alftron slid on his feet and used his extra vision to help him see through objects to escape Waglemoozone. His eyes on his fingers helped him see around corners. So that he didn't bump into the Zobtron who were evil and scary.

On his way, he met a small, weird thing that had no eyes, he wanted to help escape. Alftron got out of Waglemoozone and found a place called home with friendly monsters. Alftron and the weird small thing lived in a cave they called Zong.

Alfie Sissons (8)
Ripley Junior School, Ripley

Untitled

Tangfastic walked on his feet. He had red and blue skin and he had sharp talons. He had a head like a snake. He had a long tongue, short hair and sharp fangs. He had five eyes and he had wings like a dragon. He had big spots with stripes on his head. He had horns. He could fix anything because he had invisible powers so that he'd blend in with other colours. He would do what you told him to do and he came from Neptune.

Aaliyah Allen-Bell (8)
Ripley Junior School, Ripley

Norman's Adventure

It was a wonderful day in Albert Einstein's lab. Albert was discovering atoms and how to use electricity wisely, when just like lightning, a flash appeared. Albert felt a little puzzled by the experiment and decided to take a nap. When he was sleeping deeply, and as still as a log, two eyes formed a little French hat under Einstein's nose. Norman was born smart and mischievous. He explored the lab and found things to use on his great adventure to explore the wonderful world of Moustache Mountain and to find his worst and most devious naughty enemy, Blackbeard.

Elena Warrington Schwabe (11)
St Anselm's School, Bakewell

The Battle Of Jebel Akhdar

Drakkhar, the colossal dragon, plodded along in his camel form when he noticed some ravens terrorising citizens. Energy covered him up as he morphed back into a dragon. This alerted the ravens who flew mindlessly at Drakkhar. As they flew at him he simply killed them with one quick swipe of his tail. Using his eagle eye vision he spotted more ravens on Jebel Akhdar. As he approached the mountain the ravens ambushed him. Shooting his tail spines, he made quick work of the first wave of ravens. Drakkhar knew he could not keep this up forever.

Ben Reeves (9)
St Anselm's School, Bakewell

The Chase

Tribus was lost, surrounded by trees. There was no way out. Suddenly, there in the woods was a glow in the eye of a creature that nobody had ever seen before, except for Tribus, he tried to run, but the creature was too fast for him.
As the moon was reaching it's highest position, he could see the glint reflecting off his teeth.
Tribus was in a state of panic, and while he was panicking, the creature was closing in. Tribus knew what he had to do! He turned invisible and breathed lava all over the creature and ran back home.

Georgina Sheppard (11)
St Anselm's School, Bakewell

Sir Scare Splat

Sir Scare Splat was walking along and his friend scared him. He suddenly splattered him. He was puzzled about how he did that, but still he carried on. That night he was thinking how he did that, he thought, *do I do that when I am scared?*
So the next day he asked his friend to scare him. He did it again, he splattered green gunk everywhere, now he knows what he does when he gets scared. It was funny because he sprayed everyone. So everyone tried to scare him lots. So that is the story of Sir Scare Splat.

Tilly Gray (11)
St Anselm's School, Bakewell

The Unexpected Turnout

Triganta was sitting calmly on his star Quinton, up in space. It was very quiet up there as there was only a few of his species on the star. The problem was, Triganta wanted to explore space but he was too afraid to jump off Quinton.

One day, he decided he was going to overcome his fear. He was hanging on the tip of his home star, but all he did was stand, until, his friend gave him a push and he fell off screaming. Then suddenly, Triganta came flying up into the sky. He had grown three beautiful wings...

Joshua Nuttall (11)
St Anselm's School, Bakewell

Soul Eater Vs Fireball

I went to the dark and damp forest to have a close look at the shadows, the nasty animals that hid in the heart of the forest. The trees smiled at me, creeping me out. Suddenly I, felt some fangs going through my skin. They were as cold as ice. I felt my whole body on a kind of metamorphosis and suddenly I was a furry dragon. I heard a noise at my right and a fireball was there, standing and staring. After a hard fight. I won the ball using my new skills. I was the first furry Dragon Superhero!

Olivia Jiménez (11)
St Anselm's School, Bakewell

Smellysplat's Farts

Smellysplat was in his home town, Stink Town. It was a regular stinky day. You couldn't see a metre in front of you and worst of all, it stank, all day, every day, But lucky for Smellysplat, he did not have a nose. He knew that it was bad because of the thick green fog around him, and the large-nose monsters throwing up and wearing nose plugs. But sadly for him, he was only a baby, and monsters get noses when they get big, so when he grew up he smelt his village and he passed out.

Beatrix Larvin (11)
St Anselm's School, Bakewell

The Lonely Monster

A lonely monster, named Tom, had a lot of friends at his old school. He had two eyes and one brain in his head like a human. When he went to his new school he got picked on. He was like no other monster. He got bullied, he had no friends. He was sad, he liked a girl called Jemma, but she didn't love him much. At the end of the week he found a new boy who was alone. They became friends and they were the strongest friends ever. When the bullies came the bullies were defeated.

Colin Wilson (11)
St Anselm's School, Bakewell

Codsworth's Stuck In A Tunnel Shop!

Once there was a guy called Codsworth, he was tall and weird. He was on Jupiter, he got confused and went to a shop to get shopping. But the shops had holes, he fell down. He asked, 'Hello?'
'Hi,' Blobminster whispered. Cod couldn't see so he ran and slipped. He ran backwards and couldn't get out. Then Blob asked, 'What are you trying to do?'
'I'm trying to get out,' Cod replied.
'I thought you wanted to shop?'
'Yes I do!' he shouted.
He could not get out so he shopped and ate all day! But he still couldn't get out...

Sonny Phelan (9)
St Luke's CE Primary School, Lowton

Zapasar And The Black Hole

One day, a mystical creature called Zapasar was assigned to a secret mission. This secret mission was to fly into the black-hole that appeared when Zapasar was born. Zapasar started flapping his dragon wings and in a few seconds he was soaring through the air and then... *pop!* Zapasar went through the black-hole but appeared in a robot dimension! Robots surrounded him. He tried to scare them with his troll fangs, scorpion tail and crab hand. But they just got closer. They forced Zapasar into a building so he couldn't fly away. Suddenly, robot faces smiled sweetly together at Zapasar.

Alex Millard (9)
St Luke's CE Primary School, Lowton

Potunia And The Magical Gummy Quest

Potunia runs a sweet shop. She loves the dog sweets. Potunia is very kind and is always smiling. One day she finds herself in Imagination Land. She walks around and hears a voice whispering to her, 'To escape you must find the diamond dog gummy sweet.'

Potunia began to feel worried so she searched high and low but no sign anywhere. Suddenly, something was brightly glowing and rustling in the bushes. It was a butterfly with a nice body. It said in a quiet voice, 'I will help you Potunia.'

She slowly said 'Yes,' They searched. Would they find it?...

Ella Scott (9)
St Luke's CE Primary School, Lowton

The Toy Adventure

One day Datbird went to the shop. When Datbird was at the shop he saw some toys. They were a girl and a dog toy. He got them. They cost £86. Datbird said, '£80.'

'Yes,' the shop man said.

Datbird ran home, he got £20 then £20 then £40. It was £80. He got in his car but it was broken. He was mad and cross. Then Catman said, 'Where are your toys?'

'They're at the shop, my car is broken.'

'I can fix it,' said Catman. So Catman fixed the car. He darted to the shop and got them.

Caitlin Tegan Collins (8)
St Luke's CE Primary School, Lowton

One Day...

Once there was a little town called Unusual World of Animals.

One sunny day, a member of the Unusual World of Animals, called Stoney, met some new friends who were Mr Grasshopper, Cutie-py and Starburst. The ruler of that world was called Blob. Stoney worked for Blob and Stoney was the richest person in Unusual World of Animals. He was rich because he won the lottery which was hundred-thousand pounds, he was very happy when he won it.

One day, another person won the lottery but this time it was one hundred more. Would Stoney leave him or kill him completely?

Louise Shepherd (9)
St Luke's CE Primary School, Lowton

The Trolls And The Aliens!

One day Tippons went off to a shop. Then he got sucked in a portal. It was a troll portal, every single troll had been sucked in. They were good trolls. Tippons became friends with the King Troll, he helped him a lot. Soon a new portal appeared. Aliens came out of the portal, Ally the king of the aliens, was ferocious. Tippons used his sharp lion teeth to bite, his tail to attack and his trunk to whack them. Tippons said, 'Can we be friends please?'
'Okay,' answered Ally and then they
became friends and lived peacefully until...

Benjamin Wu (9)
St Luke's CE Primary School, Lowton

The Magical Portal

Once, in an immense colourful land, was a creature named Birdman. Birdman was very different to everyone else. Every day he walked the long way home from school.

One cold, frosty, winter day he got so cold he had to go into a bush. Then he found... a portal. It was crimson black. He then said to himself, 'Wow that is so cool.'

Then he heard a voice. 'Step into the portal, little boy.' So Birdman jumped straight into the scary portal. Then he arrived in a blink of an eye. He saw a massive, golden, beautiful, immense oak tree...

Tom Sofield (9)
St Luke's CE Primary School, Lowton

A Trip To Earth

Once, just before time on Planet Jupiter, a little alien called Zoggul Zogpants caused chaos. He was very mischievous and accidentally fell into a magic portal and went to Earth! He sat on chairs and ate. He visited the mall where a family looked after him and raised him as a human. The family had a little girl called Polly. Polly loved aliens! She played with Zoggul. Zoggul loved Polly and didn't want to leave. But, he knew the magic portal would be back soon.

One day, the magic portal came back and Zoggul left, but Polly went with him.

Olivia Barrow (9)
St Luke's CE Primary School, Lowton

A Crazy Creature Day!

One day there was a creature. This one was called Slumble. It was really friendly. He went into a chocolate shop! It was very vibrant. The shopkeeper said, 'I need help!'
'Okay,' said the creature. It went into a portal. It took him into a strange gummy land. Little gummy men were trying to build a house! It was a difficult job! The creature collected the sugar canes, chocolate wood, and so on. 'That helped a lot!' The creature went back home. He sat down and watched some of his special night TV. It was his favourite thing to do.

Anna Winterbottom (9)
St Luke's CE Primary School, Lowton

Flappy Elephant

One day Flappy Elephant who had an elephant body and bird wings, had a sore leg so he went to the walk-in centre. There was a portal so Flappy went through it because he thought it was the walk-in centre. They didn't take much time so he went with a lovely lady called Morgan. 'What do you want?' said Morgan.
Flappy Elephant said, 'My leg is sore!'
'But I'm not a nurse, I'm a school teacher,' said Morgan.
Flappy Elephant said, 'Oh no!' sounding embarrassed. 'Oh I should have stayed at home.'

Catrin Norman (9)
St Luke's CE Primary School, Lowton

Tumbles' Great Adventure

Tumbles loved eating, he would never ever stop, until one day, he saw the food delivery. Tumbles was over-excited. He quickly ran to the van and with his arms he managed to fall! The doors suddenly opened. He saw the food and he fell in a portal. Suddenly *splosh!* He landed in the sea. He had not a clue who the driver was! The first thing Tumbles saw was a very greedy shark eating some fish. Tumbles got very scared and quickly swam away. As Tumbles was swimming, 'Hello! My name is Tumble!'
'Who are you?'
'I'm yours!'

Daniel White (9)
St Luke's CE Primary School, Lowton

Candy World

In Crazytown lived a vibrant monster. He was called Bogling. He had a friend called FBFL. Bogling had wings and a spiky tail, four legs, nine eyes, horns, antennae and a mane.

One day, they were flying and they accidentally went through a portal. The world was made out of sweets, there was a chocolate jail with a sign saying: 'Danger'.

They ate some chocolate and found a chocolate bunny. They took it home, the bunny grew bigger and bigger. When they were gone it ate and smashed the house to bits then went and found the portal...

Christopher Friar (8)
St Luke's CE Primary School, Lowton

The Capture Of The Sword Of Evil

One day a horrifying creature called, Psychic Destroyer, had a very important job to go and claim the evil sword. But to get it he had to slay the poison python and go to a monster kingdom and finally get the sword of evil and become the king of monster valley. Psychic Destroyer set off and suddenly the python and Psychic Destroyer met and they had a very long battle but Psychic Destroyer grabbed hold of the poison python and stabbed it's heart. He went through the monster kingdom and went across the bridge and finally claimed the evil sword.

Harry Owen (8)
St Luke's CE Primary School, Lowton

A Bear That Has Never Seen Snow

A bear that had never seen snow before went on holiday to a sunny country. As soon as he got there, it started snowing. Snowy muttered, 'Get these things that are on me now!' Then Snowy realised it was snow. Then the only problem was he had no one to have a snowball fight with. Suddenly, there was this kid who wanted a snowball fight. Snowy said, 'I am rubbish at snowball fights.' As soon as they started having a snowball fight, Snowy hit the kid in the face. Snowy shouted, 'Ha, ha!' Then the kid hit Snowy...

Liam Bond (8)
St Luke's CE Primary School, Lowton

A New Friend In A Different Planet!

Dontastar was a kind, honest and cute animal. She had the face of a donkey, antennae's with twinkly stars on top and four fluffy legs. She went out on a walk when the sun was shining brightly. She decided to go for a swim but, the pool was a portal to a new world...

In this new world, Donastar met a friend called Skunk-Sharp Shade. He had a skunk's bottom, sharp scales, a shaded neck and very soft teeth. They played together until it was time to go home, but they may not return! They may not see each other again!

Lucy Rava (9)
St Luke's CE Primary School, Lowton

Cheetah Man

Cheetah Man had sprung into Lewis' house. He found himself in the bedroom. Cheetah Man said, 'Oh no, I have to escape this house.' Lewis spotted him and thought he was an Action Man and started to play. Cheetah Man didn't like this so he ran off into the bathroom. He didn't know where he was. But then he knew when he saw the bath. Cheetah Man hated the place because there was so much water. Water was the only thing that could kill him. He had to go far away. He finally ran out of the house of terror.

Noah Lewis (9)
St Luke's CE Primary School, Lowton

Grahammy Crazy Creature

There once lived a creature. He was called Grahammy. He was part human and dinosaur. He was scared of this land but he wanted to explore the world, but he just didn't know where to go so he just walked until he found a shop. But he didn't know it was Specsavers! Then a voice said, 'Do you want your eyes tested?'
He didn't know so he just said, 'Yes!'
Later he could see where to go. He got so excited and he wondered where he could go next. What do you think? Where could he go next...?

Evie Cass (8)
St Luke's CE Primary School, Lowton

Holly And Bob

Holly and her friend, Bob, were skipping when they heard a noise. It was a motorbike centre. They wanted to know how to ride, so they asked if they could have lessons. They started in four days. They were rubbish. They tried and tried five times. They were rubbish.
Ten days later they could do it. They could do triple jumps. But one day they forgot how to do it so they practised. They still could not remember so they took lessons again and they got the hang of it. They never forgot again and they did it forever.

Sophie Rava (9)
St Luke's CE Primary School, Lowton

The Flying Broken Leg Monster

One day the flying monster had a fall. He went to the doctor's quick and then he fell again. This time he was fine though and then he fell and broke his leg and then somebody came after him. He managed to get away. After that, he had to rest for a bit but before he knew it he was back up on his feet. He then helped anybody if needed and helped everybody if they needed it. He then kept safe and never hurt himself ever again. He was always careful not to hurt anybody again and forever more.

Sam Critchley (9)
St Luke's CE Primary School, Lowton

The Footballer Alien

One day, there was a monster called Bob. He was a footballer and was very good. He played for Liverpool. He was a striker. It was a day when he was going to play against Manchester United. As he went on the pitch, he started playing straight away, he went in for the tackle, got the ball and passed to his player and he passed back. Bob ran down the pitch and scored! It was one-nil to Liverpool.

After the game ended Liverpool all went for a very nice yummy and excellent big-sized hot dog!

Charlie Angus (9)
St Luke's CE Primary School, Lowton

Untitled

Once there was a creature called Christopholus. He had big horns.
One day, he was going to have a nice meal but when he got there he wasn't allowed in. Then he asked again, but still the same answer. Eventually, he got bored and went home.
The next day, he went back, they said the same thing and that made him angry. Then he got angrier because they told him to get lost, so he got so mad! Then he attempted to break the door. The door came down.
What happened next?

Albie Grimshaw (8)
St Luke's CE Primary School, Lowton

Getting Hurt Playing Football

Bob the monster, was very lazy and strong. A few days later... he went to a football game; he got tackled and he got hurt. When he was in the hospital he was in a cast. He hoped to get some crutches. If he got some crutches he would be so happy. He got some crutches.

A few days later was his birthday. He was so excited, it was going to be good. He wanted some Lego, an Xbox One and some Lego games and lots of books! And what a party!

Seb Scott (9)
St Luke's CE Primary School, Lowton

Back To Mars!

Crazy-Bonker lives on Planet Mars. His favourite food was Swamssole. It is a kind of rotten potato. Crazy-Bonker gazed at the stars. 'I'm going to build a rocket so I can meet Snotoscumber. My rocket is done now I have to fly to Rhubarb Land. Snotoscumber I've come to see you for the day,' said Crazy-Bonker,
'I've got a better idea, why don't you live on Mars,' said Snotoscumber.
'Brilliant idea,' said Crazy-Bonker so, they got the rocket and headed off back to Mars. Crazy-Bonker gave Snotoscumber some Swamssole.
'Thank you, I was quite peckish.' *Crunch, crunch!* Deliciously yummy.

Elise Gill (8)
Winster CE Primary School, Winster

Scwigle And Wigle!

The cup sat on the teacher's desk. Everybody thought it was empty but it wasn't.
Megan waited until everyone was gone before looking inside. She was right. She had seen something in the cup and it was looking straight at her. Two enormous green eyes blinked at her. 'Hello,' a very posh voice squeaked, 'my name is Scwigle and Wigle, pleased to meet you, I am a monster from Planet Lollipop.'
'Megan, go out to play,' said the teacher. Megan looked at her, then at the cup...
Until next time, she thought and skipped off into the spring sunshine.

Kitty Lee (8)
Winster CE Primary School, Winster

Shape-Shifter, The Snoring Octopus

Shape-Shifter was an amazing octopus who snored louder than a lion.

On 10th January, 2008, Shape-Shifter moved house to Planet Zum Zee. He was scaly, bright orange. Shape-Shifter was a secret agent on Mars. Every day he wore green for some reason.

He went to bed and started snoring. It was louder than a dog barking. It was ear-blasting! All of Zum Zee could hear it. You could hear it from another universe.

Then Heroic Bob really wanted to kill Shape-Shifter. He got to the noisy cave and went into Shape-Shifter's cave and murdered him for being too loud!

Bethany Bradley (9)
Winster CE Primary School, Winster

The Spooky Island

There was a monster called Silly Spike who lived underneath the water. His mum and dad died when he was one year old, whilst they were going to get some food. They never came back. After he became a robber, he went to get some metal. He built a time machine. Next he went back in time to kill Santa. Instead of killing Santa he saw his mum and dad dead, then he cried his eyes out. So he went back to his house. Then he waited till Christmas night. He stole the presents. He went to jail and died.

Jessica Webster (9)
Winster CE Primary School, Winster

Untitled

Flash lived on the cold planet in outer space. He ran around the cold planet all day. Some people went into outer space and the people landed on the cold planet. The people were so cold.
One person saw the creature, Flash and the creature was hungry. It ate the people. He walked off and saw the spaceship. He walked near the spaceship and he got inside. He climbed up, turned the engine on and blasted off to Earth. He landed on Earth and broke the houses and roads. He dug a hole and hid.

Logan Brown (7)
Winster CE Primary School, Winster

The Tale Of Party Monster

One day there was a monster called Party Monster. He had a cake for a body and a lollipop head. People were scared of him. He partied too much. He had a super power. One eye was a disco ball and if you looked into it, you would start dancing and never stop. With his other eye he would shoot banana skins so you would fall over and you wouldn't get up. But one day he got caught by the policeman and got put in prison for years. He got sent to Planet Snotasures forever.

Liam Crowther (9)
Winster CE Primary School, Winster

The Treacherous Adventure

T-rex took over the underworld after a battle. T-rex went to the forest. He was tired. He went to his master and told his master he saw people.
T-rex was hungry so he went to find food. T-rex ate all the food and it was lovely. T-rex went back to the moon because he missed home. He went back to his house to sleep and dream about the adventure.

Kevin Webster (7)
Winster CE Primary School, Winster

Young Writers
Est.1991

YOUNG WRITERS INFORMATION

We hope you have enjoyed reading this book – and that you will continue to in the coming years.

If you're a young writer who enjoys reading and creative writing, or the parent of an enthusiastic poet or story writer, do visit our website www.youngwriters.co.uk. Here you will find free competitions, workshops and games, as well as recommended reads, a poetry glossary and our blog.

If you would like to order further copies of this book, or any of our other titles, then please give us a call or visit www.youngwriters.co.uk.

Young Writers
Remus House
Coltsfoot Drive
Peterborough
PE2 9BF
(01733) 890066
info@youngwriters.co.uk